Spoon Rebellion

Matt Black

smith|doorstop

Published 2017 by
smith|doorstop books
The Poetry Business
Bank Street Arts
32–40 Bank Street
Sheffield S1 2DS

Copyright © Matt Black 2017
All Rights Reserved

ISBN 978-1-910367-75-9
Typeset by Camilla Lovell Design
Printed by People for Print, Sheffield

smith|doorstop books are a member of Inpress:
www.inpressbooks.co.uk. Distributed by NBN
International, 10 Thornbury Road, Plymouth, PL6 7PP

The Poetry Business gratefully acknowledges the support of
Arts Council England.

Contents

5	Field
6	No time for Xanadu
7	Knuckle
8	Dr. Hall examines the body politic
9	Susannah's remedy for the body politic
10	On Shakespeare receiving the Evaluation Forms after the First Performance of King Lear
11	River talk
12	Spoon rebellion
14	Father, forgive me
16	Swimmer
17	Grandma makes a difference
18	the cooling towers' farewell
20	Shirebrook
21	Market Street, Clay Cross
22	Bath Street, Ilkeston
23	A pint in The Sun
24	Where candle-nights flicker
25	Miles From Nowhere

Field

When I saw my bank manager last Tuesday,
he lifted his head, like he'd been grazing
in a distant meadow, and his eyes
looked through the glass at me, as if to say,

No, I am not playing the piano freestyle,
or splashing my feet across quivering marshland,
but the wife has booked us a fortnight on a beach in Croatia,
and we will be having a nice barbecue this weekend.

I wanted to tell him he was not alone,
but I could see he was, and no metaphor
was going to change him, restore him, bring him back
to the pastures of his long-lost field.

I wanted to tell him, maybe we share that field,
but he was too busy sorting my direct debits.

No time for Xanadu

I leave the screen, the urgent Inbox waiting,
budgets, bullet-points, meetings all day through –
read me, reply me, no time for friendly greeting,
always so busy, no time for Xanadu.

Because outside a gorgeous wind is blowing
through the trees, and doesn't give a damn
about the warming world, or how's the office going,
or anything I try, or who the hell I am.

The leaves on the trees are simple,
they will turn red, fall to the ground –
like love they will happen, that is real,
at least more real than anything else I've found.

I don't need the milk of Paradise, it's true –
to leave the desk and walk outside will do.

Knuckle

The black arrow on my shin points to the weakness,
this knee, where the surgeon will wield his knife.
I wait here, marked like a beast, stay calm
under the European Court of Human Rights.
Soon I'll be in theatre, it's a stage,
to bleed or not to bleed, survive the anaesthetic.
We are not sheep, this is routine surgery, not slaughter.
Matt, you are being melodramatic.

I'm wired, in a fog of nerves, where doctors prowl.
Prepped and laid out for the blade, soon I'll be asleep.
Close to being nothing but animal in gown.
Flab on slab, mound of man, free-range, fresh meat.
Now try this without smiling nurses, morphine, pills.
Try being led blind, without words, from the field.

Dr. Hall examines the body politic

The humours in our land, having lost proportion,
had fallen into fears and nightmares, excess bile,
the face of us excoriated, jaundiced Britain,
the body Scorbutick. I observed it for a while.
The South too much phlegm, the North full of choler,
Wales melancholic, only Surrey seemed sanguine,
the North East afflicted with wind and daily dolour.
To this miserable state I prescribed the following:

A clyster of rhubarb in a rear egg, thus letting
Essex be purged, and relieving the grief;
I wrapped cities in linen, made milk broth for sweating
agues, as divisions increased, from London to Leith.
By this cured, so I said, but like a monster I lied.
Blessed be God, but soon after, the Kingdom died.

---

* Dr. John Hall, 1575-1635, was a physician whose practice was based on herbs, roots, barks and purgatives to address imbalances of the four humours. He was married to Shakespeare's older daughter, Susannah.

Susannah's remedy for the body politic

John love, I don't think this country's dead at all.
Feel here, a fiscal pulse twitches, she's not broke,
she smiles and kicks, and is continent withal,
despite false gentry, and the misled groundlings' vote.
The dumbshow is over, the Leavers remain,
the head is full of poison, must be bled,
but we must work with healers, who understand the pain
in all the villages, till everyone is fed.

Such old divisions, such greed in City and Court,
and the Press must be purged with peacock dung,
but there's great love in most houses, and in the middling sort,
and armed with a sharp Fool, a new Life is begun.
John, *Heal Thyself* is the only place to start,
and 'fore prescribing for others, examine your own heart.

On Shakespeare receiving the Evaluation Forms after the First Performance of King Lear

For Shakespeare's brows knitted fiery tempests
when he was handed the evaluation forms
by his Arts Development Officer.
"Some of them disquieted? Upset?" he howled,
"Forsooth, am I writing the fen-sucked Archers?
Are these players strutting wild on this heath
as meat to merely titillate the vultures?
See here, sir – 'How did you find the venue?'
Why, full of sawdust and spit and raged upon
by a poor, bare, forked animal.
'Was the publicity easy to read?'
Ay, easy as the mind of a demented king.
No, no, no, no – no more of this.
Zounds, already my mind dreads and frets
upon the Health and Safety discussion
concerning Exit, pursued by a Bear.
Will this mountain kingdom of paper
truly change our state for better?
Will you still not offer me these boards,
this empty space, this naked stage
without the usurious stench of market?
Ay, for I challenge you, most noble officer,
tick your own boxes with your own honest answers –
agree, strongly disagree, don't mind too much,
don't care one way or another."

River talk

Leave the day-job, the land, the landed;
come with me and stand in water.
Listen to river talk, where wild currents whisper
caddis, mayfly, nymph, swirl spells
and whirlpools. Forget the photocopier.
Let the river giggle, shler,
round dolphin-nosed rocks wrinkle.

Stand silver in your cold skin, feel
the quiet ripple. Go deeper, under
shady graveyard trees, where the flow
is black and calm, glacial slow.
Let go of your love-life, and its worries.
In this dappled dome, forget home,
observe the drift of silent leaves.

Some wait here, water-waisted,
tie a dusted fly, read tiny splashes, circles,
whip their lines, zithering snakes
through the air. It seems to be a mayfly
dropping naturally. They watch it,
lift, mend the line for perfect drift,
draw feathers in the stream.

Be alone. Soft peaty orange-brown below;
the bed, the redds. Quick tail-lights flash
from wild trout, pink jewels. Be with otter,
deer, kingfisher. Be eyes and ears. Just be.
Nobody talks to you here, except the river,
and tiny ships of bubbles, floating through,
search where-are-you sea.

Spoon rebellion

    I don't know how long I've been planning spoon rebellion. Maybe it's just come over me, thinking about you once again, and carefully drying all those spoons in the cool drawers in your house. I know it's too late now, you're gone. And yes, we've wept and drunk champagne and scattered your ashes in the ocean, but it does satisfy something even now, the idea of getting drunk and spoons rebelling. Spoons up in arms leaping out of drawers, spoons laughing and jumping up and down on your polished tabletops. What would you say? Spoons doing spoony tap-dances up the walls and over the ceiling like upside-down Fred Astaires.

    But that's the way it comes over me, and it makes me giggle, when I think about solemnly drying up your spoons and putting them away under the shadow of your clenched lip. Your silence, your busy busy busy behind me in the kitchen. The spoons we must use for your family-famous puddings, gooseberry fool, windy pud, the silver spoons we are meant to be grateful for inheriting. Here they wait, in the frayed wooden drawer in the kitchen barn at the back of the old house. In the romantic south of France, where very un-romantically you have no money. And very impractically we have to travel all the way from England to even see you. And then we have to dry up those spoons so carefully.

But the wine is cheap, and it's good to be here with you. Even like this, with you busy washing up, clenched lip, thinking about your paintings and having no money and looking worried. Ok, so maybe I haven't dried them up the way you wanted, and I think I will get drunk. And in the back of my mind, yes, spoon rebellion is well begun by now. I'm twenty-three, and I have no idea what I'm doing. The pressure's on, and my tongue is about as articulate as spoons. As your own, as your own zone of silence behind me, busy busy busy, there you go. You flatten your tongue, mother, and I'll flatten mine.

Anyway, for now I'll just dry them up and put them away. Why not? After all, they're only spoons, aren't they. It's no big deal. And we'll do something different in a minute. Have a cup of coffee and talk about something jolly. Yes, that'll be better. So there they are, spoons all put away now, lying in the cool shade, next to the knives.

Father, forgive me

for like a chip off the old block
I stole a handful of your best, worn chisels
from your very last century studio, wild with ivy,
buckets, ancient oil cans, sculptures started, half-

assembled birds which now will never fly.
It was wrong, but you rarely give us presents
unless you count the endless stream of interesting but

wearing stories of artistic exploits, with confusing
allusions, subtle and less than subtle,
to multiple affairs you think clever
while we think back to our mother;

and sagas about the provenance and gallavantings
behind the curiosities, kitchenware and gee-gaws
in the rag-and-bone crazy-house shop of your heart.

So I took my own heirlooms.
As honour among thieves, as tribute
to your greed for life, your role-model training,
how best to steal plants from neighbour's gardens.

Last week you haggled with a friend,
cross but very you, grinning fiercely, charm and charisma
shining through till upstaged by your dementia.

You barter him up to two hundred readies
for three planks, stored for thirty years,
grumble you've been fleeced, smile as if you know
you haven't; slip the notes in your trouser pocket

and hobble away,
your last ten minute's work
fluttering down the path.

Swimmer

Aged sixty, I want cold water,
to slide into loose lakes, clean stroke of river,
simplicity of H_2O, to be fearless,

breathless, with white hands and toes,
in an empty quarry pool, where I jump in to freeze,
weightless but held, yelling blue across the sky;

to be swept past rocks, taken by the current,
or into the still, dark reservoir,
two brown eyes cruising the rippled mirror.

Tired of decisions, I want aquatic definition,
tight nipples, leg-thrash like ice-lightning
below the surface, unable to touch the bottom;

to disappear inside the blackness, to feel wind strike
my hair, the endless flow of animal and light,
the spirit shock and kick of being there.

Grandma makes a difference

Black flowers bloomed inside Grandpa for years
and black petals fell from his tongue.
The black stuff was squashed like a handkerchief
inside his mouth all week long.

He gnashed, and mashed, shook his teacup,
working out what was wrong;
raised his banner, printed pamphlets,
till Grandma came and sang her song.

Grandma, like a butterfly, caused thunderstorms
to rumble in remote locations.
Like a stone thrown in the pond of Wath-upon-Dearne
the ripples spread out to distant nations.

With her rituals she came, and changed the landscape,
washing floors, singing, shining the taps
to catch the light and bringing, for Grandpa and herself,
white flowers over the whitened doorstep.

the cooling towers' farewell

two dirty chef's hats, risen from the Don,
lost behind poplars, Junction 34
empty cathedrals, wearing the tides, silted,
like Cleethorpes beach risen into the sky
(smudged with oil, smeared with toil)
looking across at Meadowhall,
we've nothing to say, nothing to say

the last two pawns in a game of historical chess,
or are we King and Queen,
taller than Sheffield Town Hall,
Mum and Dad of the chimney-filled city,
we say nothing, know everything,
that steam rises, and air is all,
Bill and Ben, the Towers of Zen

on one of us, black flames like pilot lights,
on the other, ghosts of old castle doors,
Aztec runes of smoke and smirch, streaks,
criss-cross paths like lost civilisations,
Stonehenge for the carbon age,
two birds' nests in the poetics of space,
and now they can never make
King Kong And The Tinsley Cooling Towers,
muddy like the long arm of Roman Kimberworth hills
sloping down behind us

yes, we knew the East Hecla works,
Emperor of foundries, Vulcan Road,
George Cohen, Howell's, saw the last of Hadfield's,
where Robert Junior invented manganese steel, created

the 8 hour day, the age of alloys, railway tracks for the world,
spitting heat and poison, sweat and bombs and shells,
pints and snap and industrial accidents,
                            broken legs and hearts,
divorces and domestics and long nights in the pub,
everything at 1100° centigrade, Union meetings,
                       Jack and Harry,
till the last days, streets thronged,
pickets, police and workers, the national strike,
saw it all reduced to rubble,
we've nothing to say

here in our last nights
we are two grim bouncers at the door to Club Sheffield,
lonely against the purple-yellow sky,
dissolving, sad and solemn,
on the long road from the South
with lorries lumbering up the hill,
Eddie Stobart, Norbert Dentressangle, Preston's of Potto,
Willi Betz, we've seen the roads fill up
with post-industrialisation and Polish trucks

coil-pots, jugs of stillness, nearly gone,
one cloud of dust and the horizon will be
smoother, cleaner, back to Blackburn meadows,
we're ready to move on, never in the headlights,
glowing by Meadowhall sodium lamplight…

a cloud rises into the sky,
wordless, air is everything

Shirebrook

Cold top of the world,
wind sharp, flat; old goose-bumps sing
north-east Derbyshire

Grand, wide Market Square,
lift clouds, blaze sun, and you're in
Shirebrook, Italia

Café de Linda,
no questions asked, they just put
sugar in your tea

Old farming ways, cold
days require gravy, mash, big
hot steak pie dinner

That fill the gap, duck?
Yes, sure did, if my wee gap
is size of a barn

Warm humour, pie, chat
keeps out cold, sharp wind, fights off
current lack of jobs

Market Street, Clay Cross

A2B Cars, drivers wanted.
6 Berth Caravan, Skegness, all mod cons.
Allotments, apply within.
Coffee and cake at Partners Hair Salon.

England Watch, only 4 Pounds,
from G.T. Electricals.
At the I Want Pet Foods Ground, Mill Lane, Holmgate,
The 2014 Fireworks Spectacle.

Friday, Andy J, Fantastic Male Vocalist,
Monday, Psychic Supper with Trisha.
Circus Wonderland presents, For One Week Only,
                            Angel and Viktoria,
Precarious Plate Spinners from Bulgaria.

Bath Street, Ilkeston

Braided hair waitress,
neat, Swiss-style, but more modern –
Heidi with tattoos

It's so red, in't it?
I only went for highlights –
well, what do you do?

To let: good shop space.
Last use, magic transactions –
Greek isle of Argos

Mini-market's gone –
I don't know why we came back
from Australia

In stone-age café,
three witches, two druids drink
Americanos

Toothless man waves fork,
laughing, opposite toothless
baby waving spoon

Old mining country –
out of work Barry wears blue
Superman t-shirt

A pint in The Sun

I'm in a red-brick palace, The Sun Inn, Eastwood,
top of the hill, third sweet pint of Corby,
drinking with a stern D.H. Lawrence, while we watch
Olympiakos versus Chelsea, on the big screen
which Lawrence has finally got used to, though he's still disturbed
by Facebook, Twitter, Grindr. He's already told me
that the room is full of men and women grateful and merciful
that history's moved on. *Yes,* I say, *except for John Terry,*
who could really do with a return to old form.
DH knocks back another double, looks from underneath
his eagle eyebrows, asks me what I know about
form, or passion. I reply, *I do my best,*
he said, *That's not how I wrote Snake or Figs,*
doing best. I burned, I sacrificed my soul.
And he bangs on and on, right through to post-match
Mourinho. I defend my rhythms, but finally give in,
he's on home turf, after all, in these soft hills
where his playing days, kissing days were born.
I want to make him smile, buy him another double,
DH, for me, you are the only Special One.

Where candle-nights flicker

Imagine the valley before the mill,
the river's rush with its own free will.
Here comes the wheel, here come the people.

A nightshirt glows under a calico moon;
a man sings Constant Employment, a new tune
weaves a poor village a utopian dream.

A school, and dancing, ale and enjoyment,
your needs looked after and holiday laughter –
the rest of the year, work hard and be sober.

Six hundred candle-nights flicker, and fall,
the call of the mill-bell, the new money spell,
the turn of the wheel that never stands still.

Imagine a mill he built like a castle,
throb of its thumb, hum of its leather,
bobbin and spindle, whirring and clatter.

Raindrops fall in a valley monsoon
on a yellow sari in the Indian sun,
where hot cotton sleeps in blossom.

Cotton dust cloud at four in the morning,
children and women, roving and reeling,
shuttle calling ...*the future, the future...*

Miles From Nowhere

In this cottage each Friday ten fine men gather,
chat cheerfully around this old wood-burner,
their aim, true as a narrowboat's lines,
to maintain, keep fit for use in these changing times
these boats, this Basin, this slow stretch of water,
so quiet beside the Industrial Quarter,
Lidl, Asda, Langley Mill, the filling station.
Sitting here, warm and safe, talking all things global,
clutching tea and doughnuts, these ten men huddle.

At its top, this old giant, Erewash Canal
sleeps under the main road by Langley Bridge Lock.
I walk into country from this suburban calm,
past young anglers on some education programme,
past dog-walkers, joggers, locals who stroll
by the milky green, where the mallards paddle,
along this towpath where native hawthorns grow.
Inspector Morse murders, a place of fear, bodies,
once they threw the lock-keeper's cottage in here,
still they pull out motorbikes, trolleys, rusty cars,
a wheelchair, that's a story, and who knows, shooting stars.

Sweat and shovels, picks and barrows, built by thousands
of navvies, their true name navigators,
with lives lost to cold and drink, slipped banks,
for what? A bad name, ill-health and little thanks.
Twelve miles, fifteen locks, and eighteen months to build
this channel lined with clay, which cattle puddled.
I watch this flat water, once free and wild
when it sparkled from the sky, cascaded down the hill
to here, in pounds, controlled, held back,
an efficient road to carry cloth and coal;
forgotten England, a better world (never really true).

A narrowboat with painted jugs, yellow, red, and blue,
flowerpots on the flat roof with dog and bike,
TV aerial, broom, single bag of coal (ironic).
Her rudder is a swan, she'll chug along, her song –
This is the life, this is what we're after,
you're free, in a world that seems richer.
The heart in a kinder space, opened up, more yourself.
Leisure-boats Josephine, Electra, Gone Roaming,
and tiny paddle boats called moorhens swim downstream;
this place of slow, slow, slow, this Arcadian path,
past industries' brickwork and its rosy glow.

Fifty yards, a different story, the Nottingham canal.
Disused, little water, stagnant green and brown,
where bulrushes rise, memorials to what has been,
like spent fireworks, where empty lager-cans lie
holding some poor kid's dreams fallen from the sky.

Under trees a big horse, industry-muscled,
whose great-great-grandfather pulled barges
                            through the night,
stalks through dishevelled willow, elder, bramble.
In a field, a farmer has set out red traffic barriers,
picked up cheap, for a makeshift gymkhana.
This graveyard finishes half a mile along,
where open cast mining in its turn has gone.
Now it's a cyclepath, for that healthy, feel-good feeling.
Canals are like running stitch round here,
under fields, roads, years, appear and disappear.

Turn right, under a bridge flows sweet River Erewash
loose and wild, through meanders, pools and oxbows,
fast flashes, quiet swirls, and that sea-like smell.
To Shipley Lock, up to MFN (Miles From Nowhere)
pub entertainment venue, with its paint-peeled door,
Welcomes Bikers and Cruisers – what sort, I don't know.
I wander round the back, two big blokes come out –
*Can we help yer? Yes, who are these figures
 on the roof? They're just Indians, mate,
from American Adventure.* In the Midlands
Pocahontas, Sitting Bull, in this cold reservation,
outside this night-club, used to be stables on a proud farm,
where bikers now get pissed round dirty tables;
and late-night drinkers slur *What's left round here?
Coal, canal, lace? There's nowt left but beer.
They took it all, the Thatcher years. All gone.*
Sitting Bull smiles, says *Nothing last long,
and when was earth ever still, or fine?*
I leave, climb the bridge above the Great Northern Line,

stand in the breeze where Knighton, Jack, Jordan,
drew a swastika, and their names, graffitied in jet black,
under the same old, same old dappled sky.

Time to move on, leave this state-of-the-nation riddle.
I walk back down to boating world, that old English idyll
where the leisured, all relaxed, lean on lock-gates
which open like wings, magpie black and white,
as we steer, and wind, and rope our passage
                                  through the flight.
In darkening locks, as the waters fall, we feel
that sinking feeling, have to touch the wall.
There's rules and laws, don't be surprised to hear, *Hey cock,
you didn't close the paddles when you left the lock.*
Cuts and weirs, boatyards, red-brick cottages,
and the unwritten law, as you approach those low bridges,
1 lad is ok, 2 lads take care, 3 lads trouble,
if they shout *Water-gypsies!* or *Wankers!* steer to the middle.
Locking up, locking down, every day's another odyssey
to the next pub, a good pint and tell another story.

Back to the young anglers, for whom the past looks dark,
only interested, or not, in bream, roach, fat carp.
Past old man's beard blossoming over barbed wire,
past a fence with doggy-doo bags hung like purple flowers.
A rusty 50 on a post, where a fisherman
                                  cast his line and stared,
remembering last night's luck, her clean hair.
Emerald-green head, a mallard on a branch, sits
mid-stream, where the beech-leaves dance.

Over the yellow teapot, in the small cottage,
welder, baker, chemist, discuss what is what –
All these floods... you can't just mess with Nature...
textile equipment... all sold to America and Asia.
But they allus meet each Friday, never mind the weather.
Talk the next canal stretch, though blocked by the A610,
but they'll get it back one day, who knows when.
They understand water, know currents,
                              rivers on their hands,
drink tea, navigate Fridays with big plans.
As they say, *If you want moon to sing, it's a wait,*
but while it's ever shining, we're all raight.

Acknowledgements

Many thanks to everyone who has given feedback on poems and encouragement; in particular Cathy Grindrod, Jim Caruth and Matt Clegg.

Many thanks to project managers, editors and others who helped the following poems to fruition or first publication.

'Field' first published in *The Animal Gaze* (smith|doorstop, 2014) anthology; 'Dr. Hall examines' and 'Susannah's remedy' from being Shakespeare Birthplace Trust Writer-in-Residence 2016; 'River talk' commissioned by Charles Monkhouse and Derwent Pulse, with thanks for inspiration from members of Derwent Fly Fishing Club; 'Spoon rebellion' published in *Ink, Sweat and Tears* online magazine; 'Father, forgive me' in *Envoi* magazine; 'Swimmer' in *The Rialto* magazine; 'Grandma makes a difference' in *Envoi* magazine; 'the cooling towers' farewell' in *The Imagined City* (smith|doorstop) anthology, and became a sound version CD with music by The Only Michael; 'Shirebrook' and 'Market Street, Clay Cross' from being First Art Writer-in-Residence 2014, and first published in *The North* magazine; 'Bath Street, Ilkeston', 'A pint in The Sun' and 'Miles From Nowhere' (thanks for inspiration from Erewash Canal Preservation Society) from being Writer-in-Residence at Changing Landscapes, run by Kate Le Prevost and the King George Gallery, Ilkeston and appeared first in the Lally Gallery, Erewash Museum; 'Where candle-nights flicker' was commissioned by Sinfonia Viva, Derby for O How That Valley Did Change, and won 1st Prize in the Buxton Poetry Festival.